Jim Henson's ANIMAL SHOW™

Horns, Tusks & Antlers

Steve Pollock

BBC CHILDREN'S BOOKS

Hi! I'm Stinky the skunk and this is Jake the polar bear from *The Animal Show*. This book is all about animals that have horns, tusks or antlers. Here are some of the guests from our show who can tell you a little about their horns, tusks or antlers.

I'm Rocky, a bighorn sheep from the Rocky Mountains of America. My horns help me to fight.

I'm Bubba and I'm a walrus. My tusks are really just big teeth for scaring other male walruses.

I'm Robert the red deer. These are my antlers. I grow a new set each year. I need them to fight off other deer who want to take my herd.

△ *Cape buffalo from East Africa*

Some types of cows, goats and sheep that live on farms have horns. They all have cousins living in the wild too.

This buffalo from Africa is part of the cattle family, just like the cow. A farmer likes cows to have small horns, not big ones like this buffalo, because big horns can be dangerous. How would you like to milk this big buffalo?

Bighorn sheep ram △

Tell us about your horns, Rocky.

I'm a bighorn sheep from the Rocky Mountains in America. When I was a baby I didn't have any horns. But as I grew I began to grow horns too. My horns have nearly finished growing. The photo shows a grown up male, a ram, with a really big set of horns.

◁ *Ibex*

Horns come in all shapes and sizes. The ibex is a kind of mountain goat with very long horns. These long horns send a message to other ibex: "be careful, my long horns are dangerous." Most of the time the ibex get the message and leave each other alone. But like a lot of other animals with horns, they will use them for fighting – but only when they have to.

Giraffe △

Giraffes' horns are different from the horns of other animals. Our horns are covered with skin and they have tufts of hair on them. Baby giraffes are born with little horns. Male giraffes use their horns for fighting each other.

Gazelles fighting △

Why do animals with horns always seem to fight, Jake?

Tommy here can explain, can't you, Tommy?

Some animals, usually the males, fight each other for food, shelter and for females to make their herds big. Although they look dangerous, horns help to stop us gazelles really hurting each other. Look how those two gazelles fight. They are using their horns to push against each other. The gazelle which pushes the hardest wins, and the loser moves away unhurt.

Bighorn sheep fighting △

When bighorn sheep fight they bang their horns together hard. The noise it makes is very loud. But like the gazelles, the strongest one wins the fight and no one is really hurt.

Herd of musk oxen △

Animals use horns to defend themselves too. Most of the time a musk ox uses its horns for pushing away other musk oxen. But when a herd of musk oxen is under attack from a pack of wolves, the musk oxen use their horns to protect themselves. They stay together in a circle, and the big ones on the outside keep the little ones safe behind them inside the circle. If a wolf comes close, the big ones use their horns to fight it off. Even when they're fighting, the big musk oxen do not leave the circle.

Horns are made from something called *keratin* like our fingernails, but they are much harder and much stronger. Underneath the horn is a bone which grows out of the head. It is this bone which makes the horns so strong. In this highland cattle bull the bones are very long.

Highland cattle bull ▽

I'm Harry the rhinoceros. As you can see, I have my horns on the end of my nose, not on the top of my head like a lot of other animals. My horn is quite different from the horns of cattle and sheep. There is no bone under it and it is made from the same substance as hair, but of course it is much stronger. We use our horns to fight each other if another rhino gets too close. We push against each other with our horns, and eventually the loser walks away. Using our horns to fight like this means we don't get hurt.

▽ *Rhino showing horn*

White rhino wallowing in mud △

That horn of ours makes a good weapon to scare off other animals, so they leave us alone. You'll have to agree that our horn and our huge size make us look pretty scary! Although our horn is a good weapon, some people hunt us rhinos for it. Now nearly all rhinos are endangered animals and we need to be protected. We're just harmless creatures who like to wallow in mud.

◁ *African elephant*

Elephant tusks like mine are really just a pair of very long front teeth. We use them when we feed to tear the bark from trees, and they make very good spades for digging up roots in the ground. Like animals with horns, we sometimes use our tusks for fighting each other.

Many elephants have really big tusks. Some older elephants have tusks as long as 2.3 metres, which is much longer than the height of an average person.

There are some differences between African and Indian elephants. Can you see what they are? Look at the shape of the head. Which one has the largest ears?

Indian elephant ▷

I'm Bubba the walrus and like Jake, I live in the cold seas of the Arctic. My tusks are teeth like an elephant's tusks, but I do not use them to feed. Like animals with horns my tusks say something about me. When they are really big, they tell other walruses who's the boss.

Walruses on a beach △

Close-up of warthog's snout ▷

We warthogs have long teeth that have grown into tusks. They are not as big as a walrus's or an elephant's tusks. We use them as weapons, but we do not use them for feeding. Any digging around in the ground is done using the hard top of the nose. The warts on a warthog's nose, which don't make us look very pretty, are there to protect us when we get into a fight.

Your horns are spiky, Robert.

Red deer with antlers 'in velvet' △

Yes they are Stinky, but they aren't called horns. These are my antlers. They are different from horns because they fall off each year when we have finished with them. Then, next year, we grow a new set. See this deer with a soft skin called velvet around his antlers. It feels just like velvet too.

Red deer with antlers exposed ▷

Once a year, at the start of the mating season, the velvet starts to peel off our antlers. We scrape the velvety skin off on trees and rocks until only the hard, bony part of the antlers is left. Guess what we use our antlers for then? Turn the page to find out.

△ *Red deer stags fighting*

You guessed it. Deer use their antlers for fighting. You can see that we lock our antlers together and push hard against each other. The strongest wins the battle and he will keep the herd of females together. When the mating season is over, the male sheds his antlers and the cycle starts all over again.

*Woman holding ▷
single deer antler*

This person has picked up one of the deer antlers that has fallen off. Sometimes we deer eat the antlers. Very crunchy! Each year an extra set of points grows on the antlers, so if you count the points on a red deer's antlers, you may be able to work out its age. This one belonged to a seven year old deer. How old am I?

△ *Kudu*

Well, Jake, I used to think that animals used horns, tusks and antlers just to fight off other animals that wanted to eat them. I didn't know they did so many things.

That's right, Stinky. What amazes me is that although they look sharp and fierce, they can save animals a lot of pain when they fight each other. And I didn't know that in some animals like the kudu, only the males have horns. You can tell this kudu is a male because of his horns.

I suppose that horns, tusks and antlers are kind of special for those animals that have them. Do you think they'd suit me?

Stinky, I don't think anyone's ever heard of a skunk with tusks!

Oh, well, I'll stick to my amazing smell instead.

Picture Credits

All wildlife photographs supplied by **Oxford Scientific Films** and credited to:
Anthony Bannister page 17; **Martyn Colbeck** page 14; **Lon E. Lauber** pages 10 and 16;
Tom Leach page 12; **Okapia** page 15; **Stan Osolinski** page 13; **Press-tige Pictures** page 11;
Frank Scneidermeyer page 22; **Survival** pages 4 (Mary Plage), 6 (Michel Strebino), 18
(William Paton), 19 (John Harris), 20 (William Paton) and 21 (Richard and Julia Kemp);
David Thompson page 7; **Steve Turner** page 8; **Tom Ulrich** front cover, pages 5 and 9.

Published by BBC Children's Books
a division of BBC Worldwide Publishing
a subsidiary of BBC Worldwide Limited
Woodlands, 80 Wood Lane, London W12 0TT

First published 1996
Text and design copyright © BBC Children's Books 1996
Based on the television series *Jim Henson's Animal Show* copyright © Jim Henson Productions, Inc. 1996
Muppet character photos and illustrations copyright © 1996 Jim Henson Productions, Inc.
Jim Henson's Animal Show with Stinky and Jake logo and character names and likenesses
are trademarks of Jim Henson Productions, Inc. All rights reserved.

ISBN 0 563 40451 5

Typeset by BBC Children's Books
Cover printed by Clays Ltd, St Ives plc
Colour separations by DOT Gradations, Chelmsford
Printed and bound in Great Britain by Cambus Litho, East Kilbride